HODDER
GRAPHICS

John Steinbeck

OF MICE AND MEN

EDITED AND ILLUSTRATED BY
Philip Page

Hodder Headline's policy is to use papers that are natural, renewable and recyclable products and made from wood grown in sustainable forests. The logging and manufacturing processes are expected to conform to the environmental regulations of the country of origin.

Orders: please contact Bookpoint Ltd, 130 Milton Park, Abingdon, Oxon OX14 4SB. Telephone: (44) 01235 827720. Fax: (44) 01235 400454. Lines are open 9.00 – 5.00, Monday to Saturday, with a 24-hour message answering service. Visit our website at www.hoddereducation.co.uk

Copyright of original text from *Of Mice and Men* © 1937 by John Steinbeck
Copyright of text and illustrations in this edition © Philip Page, 2007
First published in 2007 by
Hodder Murray, an imprint of Hodder Education,
a member of the Hodder Headline Group, an Hachette Livre UK Company,
338 Euston Road
London NW1 3BH

Impression number	5 4 3 2
Year	2010 2009 2008 2007

Cover photo © Bettmann/Corbis
Typeset in Adobe Garamond 13pt by DC Graphic Design Limited, Swanley Village, Kent
Printed and bound in Great Britain by Martins The Printers, Berwick-upon-Tweed

A catalogue record for this title is available from the British Library

ISBN: 978 0340 928 653

Contents

About the story

George and Lennie are two unskilled labourers travelling around California in search of work in the 1930s, a time of high unemployment and poverty in the USA. Like many others, they dream of having their own farm and working for themselves, and this time their dream — the so-called 'American Dream' — might just come true! But Lennie, in spite of his tremendous strength, only has the mind of a child and is always getting into trouble — and there is plenty of that waiting for them on the ranch in the Salinas Valley.

Steinbeck took the title of his story from a poem by the Scottish poet Robert Burns: 'the best laid plans o' mice an' men, Gang aft agley [go wrong]'. In the story, Steinbeck explores themes such as loneliness and friendship, hope and despair, kindness and cruelty, racism and the different ways people use power over others. Look out for these themes as you read the story and notice the sympathetic way the author writes about people many might describe as 'losers'.

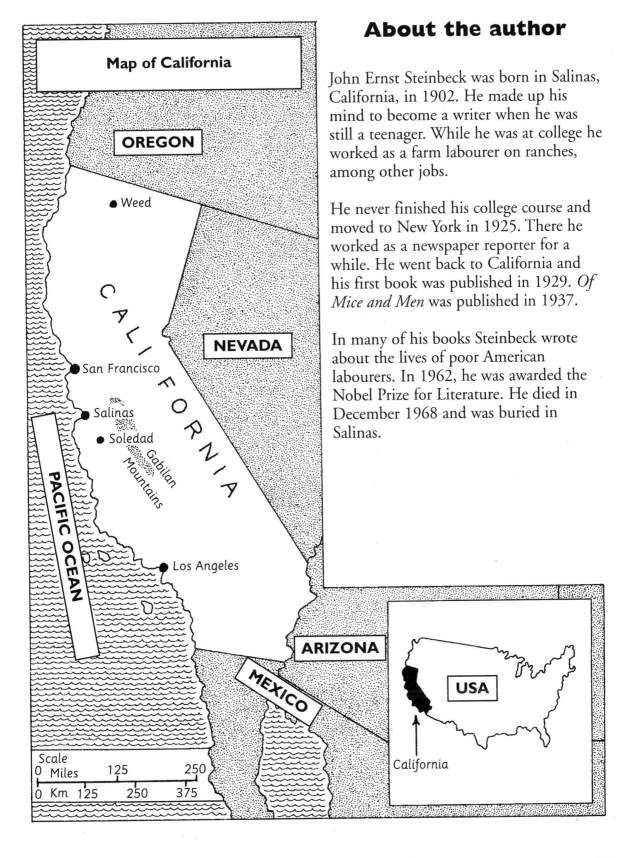

Map of California

OREGON

Weed

CALIFORNIA

NEVADA

San Francisco

Salinas

Soledad

Gabilan Mountains

PACIFIC OCEAN

Los Angeles

ARIZONA

MEXICO

USA

California

Scale

0 Miles   125   250

0 Km 125   250   375

About the author

John Ernst Steinbeck was born in Salinas, California, in 1902. He made up his mind to become a writer when he was still a teenager. While he was at college he worked as a farm labourer on ranches, among other jobs.

He never finished his college course and moved to New York in 1925. There he worked as a newspaper reporter for a while. He went back to California and his first book was published in 1929. *Of Mice and Men* was published in 1937.

In many of his books Steinbeck wrote about the lives of poor American labourers. In 1962, he was awarded the Nobel Prize for Literature. He died in December 1968 and was buried in Salinas.

Cast of characters

George Milton
A migrant (travelling)
labourer

Lennie Small
George's simple-minded
friend

The boss
The ranch owner

Curley
The boss's son – a small,
bad-tempered man

Curley's wife
A lonely young woman
who flirts with the men

Candy
The old 'swamper'
(cleaner)

Crooks
The 'stable buck' who looks
after the horses and mules

Slim
A wagon driver and the most
respected ranch worker

Carlson

Whit

Ranch workers

George and Lennie camp for the night before they go to the ranch to work. George gives Lennie some important instructions!

A few miles south of Soledad, the Salinas River drops in close to the hillside bank and runs deep and green. On one side the golden foothill slopes up to the Gabilan mountains, but on the valley side the water is lined with trees – willows fresh and green with every spring, and sycamores. There is a path through the willows beaten hard by boys coming down from the ranches to swim and by tramps who come wearily down from the highway.

Evening of a hot day started a little wind among the leaves. On the sand banks rabbits sat as quietly as little gray, sculptured stones.

From the direction of the highway came the sound of footsteps. The rabbits hurried for cover. A heron labored up into the air and pounded down river. For a moment the place was lifeless, then two men walked down the path.

The first man was small and quick with restless eyes and sharp features. Behind walked his opposite, a huge man, shapeless of face, dragging his feet the way a bear drags his paws.

The first man stopped. His huge companion flung himself down and drank from the green pool with long gulps, snorting into the water like a horse.

Lennie, for God's sake don't drink so much. You gonna be sick like you was last night.

Tha's good. You drink some, George.

Tastes all right. You never oughta drink water when it ain't running, Lennie. You'd drink out of a gutter if you was thirsty.

He threw a scoop of water into his face and rubbed it about with his hand, under his chin and around the back of his neck. Then he replaced his hat, pushed himself back, drew up his knees and embraced them. Lennie, who had been watching, imitated George exactly.

We could of rode clear to the ranch if that bastard bus driver knew what he was talkin' about. Too God damn lazy to pull up.

Kicks us out and says, 'Jes' a little stretch down the road.' I bet it was <u>more</u> than four miles.

George? Yeah, what ya want?

Where we goin', George?

So you forgot that awready, did you?

I tried not to forget. Honest to God I did, George.

OK – OK. Might jus' as well spen' all my time tellin' you things and then you forget and I tell you again.

● Why does Lennie imitate George?

I remember about the rabbits, George.

To hell with the rabbits. That's all you ever can remember is them rabbits.

Now listen and this time you got to remember so we don't get in no trouble.

You remember they gave us **work cards** and bus tickets?

Oh, sure, George. I remember that now.

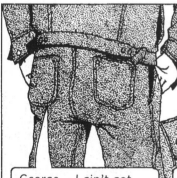

George... I ain't got mine. I musta lost it.

I got both of 'em here.

What'd you take outa that pocket? What you got in your hand?

Nothin', George. Honest.

Give it here.

It's on'y a mouse, George. Jus' a dead mouse. I didn't kill it. Honest! I found it dead.

Give it here!

Lennie's closed hand slowly obeyed. George took the mouse and threw it across the pool.

work cards — permits issued by a government agency to provide jobs

What would you want of a dead mouse, anyways?

I could **pet** it with my thumb while we walked.

Well, you ain't petting no mice while you walk with me. You remember where we're goin' now?

I forgot again.

Jesus Christ. We're gonna work on a ranch like the one we come from up north. We're gonna go in an' see the boss. I'll give him the work tickets, but you ain't gonna say a word.

If he finds out what a crazy bastard you are, we won't get no job, but if he sees you work before he hears ya talk, we're set. Ya got that?

Sure, George. Sure I got it.

I ain't gonna say nothin'... I ain't gonna say nothin'... I ain't gonna say nothin'.

OK. An' you ain't gonna do no bad thing like you done in Weed, neither.

Like I done in Weed?

Forgot that too? Well I ain't gonna remind ya, fear ya do it again.

pet — stroke

• Lennie likes to stroke things. What 'bad thing' might he have done in Weed?

A light of understanding broke on Lennie's face.

They run us outta Weed.

Run us out, hell. We run. They was lookin' for us, but they didn't catch us.

I didn't forget that, you bet.

George lay back and crossed his hands under his head, and Lennie imitated him, raising his head to see whether he was doing it right. The day was going fast now. Only the tops of the mountains flamed with the light of the sun. A water snake slipped along the pool, its head like a little periscope.

George — ain't we gonna have no supper?

Sure. I got three cans of beans in my **bindle**.

You gather up some dead willow sticks. I'll give you a match. Then we'll heat the beans and have supper.

I like beans with ketchup.

Well, we ain't got no ketchup. You go get wood.

Lennie lumbered to his feet and disappeared. There were sounds of splashings down the river in the direction Lennie had taken. In a moment Lennie came crashing back through the brush. He carried one small willow stick in his hand.

bindle — a 'bundle' of personal belongings rolled up in a blanket

Awright. Gi'me that mouse!

What mouse, George? I ain't got no mouse.

I don't know why I can't keep it. It ain't nobody's mouse. I didn't steal it.

George threw the mouse as far as he could and washed his hands. He heard Lennie's whimpering cry.

I ain't takin' it away jus' for meanness. You get another that's fresh and I'll let you keep it.

I don't know where there is no other mouse. I remember a lady used to give 'em me. But that lady ain't here.

That was your own Aunt Clara. An' she stopped givin' 'em to ya. You always killed 'em.

They was so little. I'd pet 'em, and pretty soon they bit my fingers and I pinched their heads a little and then they was dead — because they was little.

I wish't we'd get the rabbits soon, George. They ain't so little.

The hell with the rabbits. An' you ain't to be trusted with no live mice. Your Aunt Clara give you a rubber mouse and you wouldn't have nothing to do with it.

It wasn't no good to pet.

Dusk came into the valley.

You gonna get that wood?

George undid his bindle and brought out three cans of beans. He stood them about the fire, not quite touching the flame.

There's enough beans for four men.

George loses his temper with Lennie and says how he would be better off without him. He describes what happened in Weed.

Read the following passage of text in your copy of the novel and then think about the questions below and the key quotes in bold.

> Lennie watched him from over the fire. He said patiently, 'I like 'em with ketchup.'
> 'Well, we ain't got any,' George exploded...
>
> ...His anger left him suddenly. He looked across the fire at Lennie's anguished face, and then looked ashamedly at the flames. "

 Think About It

1 Look again at page 7. How does George know that Lennie went to look for the dead mouse?

2 George keeps telling Lennie what to do all the time. Does this mean he is naturally bossy?

3 **God a'mighty, if I was alone I could live so easy.**

George describes to Lennie what he could do if he was 'alone' – take his 'fifty bucks' (50 dollars, his month's wages) and to go town to play cards or pool, order dinner, drink whisky or even stay in a 'cat house' (brothel). This would probably use up all of his wages and he would be back at the ranch with nothing to show for his month's work.

Do you think George really wants to lead this sort of life? Or is he just frustrated with being 'tied down' by Lennie?

When you have finished the book, look back at George's statement here. Does he still think this?

4 **Jus' wanted to feel that girl's dress – jus' wanted to pet it like it was a mouse.**

What did the girl think that Lennie was doing? How did she react?

Why did George and Lennie have to hide in a ditch all day? (When George says they had to 'get outta the country' he means the area, or town, not the USA.)

5 George is ashamed after he has said **'I wisht I could put you in a cage.'** Later in the book, this is a real threat to Lennie – see page 38 where Crooks threatens him with 'the booby hatch' and page 49 where Carlson says what will happen to Lennie if caught.

George?

Whatta you want?

I was only foolin', George. I don't want no ketchup. I wouldn't eat no ketchup if it was right here beside me.

When I think of the swell time I could have without you, I go nuts. I never get no peace.

George, you want I should go away? I could go off in the hills there. I'd find a cave.

Yeah? How'd you eat? You ain't got sense enough to find nothing to eat.

I'd find things, George. I don't need no nice food with ketchup. I'd lay in the sun and nobody'd hurt me. An' if I foun' a mouse, I could keep it.

I been mean, ain't I?

I was jus' foolin', Lennie. 'Cause I want you to stay with me.

I want you to stay with me, Lennie. Somebody'd shoot you for a **coyote** if you was by yourself. Your Aunt Clara wouldn't like you running off by yourself, even if she is dead.

I can go away any time.

Tell you what I'll do. First chance I'll give you a pup. Maybe you wouldn't kill *it*.

coyote — a type of wolf

10

Lennie persuades George to describe the dream they both share. He never gets tired of hearing it and how they will live 'off the fat of the land' on their own small farm.

Read the following passage of text in your copy of the novel and then think about the questions below and the key quotes in bold.

> Lennie spoke craftily, 'Tell me – like you done before.'
> 'Tell you what?'
> 'About the rabbits.'...
>
> ...He drove his knife through the top of one of the bean cans, sawed out the top and passed the can to Lennie. Then he opened a second can. From his side pocket he brought out two spoons and passed one of them to Lennie.

 Think About It

1 Lennie says that ketchup is 'nice food'. What does this remark tell you about the sort of life he and George lead?

2 On page 10, George says that he wants Lennie to stay with him. Why would George say this, if Lennie keeps getting them both into trouble?

3 **'Guys like us, that work on ranches, are the loneliest guys in the world.'**

George describes how ranch workers are usually alone, come to a ranch and 'work up a stake' (earn some money) but then waste it in town. George and Lennie have each other, and don't have to sit in a bar spending their money because they've nowhere else to go. 'We got a future.'

Think about what George said earlier about being alone. (See the passage of text referred to on page 9 **'God a'mighty, if I was alone I could live so easy.'**) Do you think he meant what he said then?

4 George and Lennie's dream is to **'live off the fatta the lan''** (live comfortably off what they can grow themselves).

Their dream is to have a little house, a few acres of land, a cow, some pigs, a garden, rabbits in cages (which Lennie will look after) chickens, a vegetable patch, a big stove ... Which part of the dream is most important to Lennie? Why?

5 George and Lennie eating beans from a can shows the reality of their lives. They dream of comfort, shelter and independence, none of which they have at the moment. Perhaps that is why George suddenly says 'Nuts!' and stops talking about it.

They sat by the fire and filled their mouths with beans.

What you gonna say tomorrow when the boss asks you questions?

I... I ain't gonna... say a word.

Good boy! That's fine, Lennie! Maybe you're gettin' better.

Look, Lennie. I want you to look around here. You can remember this place can't you?

Sure, I can remember this.

If you jus' happen to get in trouble like you always done before, I want you to come right here an' hide in the **brush**.

Hide in the brush till I come for you. Can you remember that?

Sure I can, George. Hide in the brush till you come.

But you ain't gonna get in no trouble, because if you do, I won't let you tend the rabbits.

The red light dimmed on the coals.

brush — wooded area

The **bunk house** was a long, rectangular building. Inside, the walls were whitewashed and the floor unpainted. Against the walls were eight bunks. Over each bunk there was nailed an apple box that made two shelves for the personal belongings of the occupant of the bunk. In the middle of the room stood a big table littered with playing cards, and around it were boxes for the players to sit on.

The boss was expectin' you last night. He was sore as hell when you wasn't here to go out this morning.

You can have them two beds there.

George leaned over and inspected the **sacking** closely. Lennie did the same. George unrolled his bindle and put things on the shelf, his razor and bar of soap, his comb and bottle of pills. Then he made his bed up neatly with blankets.

bunk house — sleeping quarters for the workers
sacking — bed covering

swamper — cleaner

I guess the boss'll be out here in a minute. He was sure **burned** when you wasn't here this morning. An' he gave the stable buck hell, too.

The stable buck?

Sure. Ya see the stable buck's a nigger. Nice fella. Got a crooked back where a horse kicked him. He reads a lot. Got books in his room.

The door opened. The boss stepped into the room with the short, quick steps of a fat-legged man.

You was to be here for work this morning.

Bus driver give us **a bum steer**. We hadda walk ten miles.

Where you boys been working?

Up around Weed.

You too?

Yeah, him too.

He ain't much of a talker, is he?

No, he ain't, but he's sure a hell of a good worker. Strong as a bull.

Why don't you let him answer? What **stake** you got in this guy? You takin' his pay away from him?

burned — angry

a bum steer — misled/tricked us
stake — interest

No. Why ya think I'm sellin' him out?

I never seen one guy take so much trouble for another guy.

He's my... cousin. I told his old lady I'd take care of him. He's awright. Just ain't bright.

Well, he don't need brains to **buck barley bags**. But don't you try to put nothing over. I got my eye on you. I seen wise guys before.

Go out with the grain teams after dinner. They're pickin' up barley at the threshing machine. Go out with Slim's team.

Now he's got his eye on us. We got to be careful and not make no slips.

You said I was your cousin, George.

Well, that was a lie. An' I'm damn glad it was. If I was a relative of yours I'd shoot myself.

The old man came into the room. At his heels there walked a drag-footed sheep dog, gray of muzzle and with pale, blind old eyes. The dog struggled lamely to the side of the room and lay down, grunting softly to himself and licking his grizzled moth-eaten coat.

buck barley bags — lift sacks of barley
grizzled — grey

15

I wasn't listening. I jus' come. I didn't hear nothing.

A guy on a ranch don't never listen nor he don't ast no questions.

That's a hell of an old dog.

Yeah, I had 'im ever since he was a pup. God, he was a good sheep-dog when he was younger.

At that moment a young man came into the bunk house. He wore a work glove on his left hand, and, like the boss, he wore high-heeled boots.

Seen my old man?

He was here jus' a minute ago, Curley. Went over to the cook house, I think.

You the new guys the old man was waitin' for?

We just come in.

Let the big guy talk.

S'pose he don't want to talk?

By Christ, he's gotta talk when he's spoke to. What the hell are you gettin' into it for?

We travel together.

Oh, so it's that way.

Yeh, it's that way.

An' you won't let the big guy talk, is that it?

He can talk if he wants to tell you anything.

We jus' come in.

Well, nex' time you answer when you're spoke to.

George watched him out, and then he turned back to the swamper.

What the hell's he got on his shoulder? Lennie didn't do nothing to him.

Well — tell you what. Curley's like a lot of little guys. He hates big guys. He's alla time picking scraps with big guys.

I seen plenty tough little guys. But this Curley better not make no mistakes about Lennie. This Curley punk is gonna get hurt if he messes around with Lennie.

Candy tells George about Curley and how he has become even more bad-tempered since he got married.

Read the following passage of text in your copy of the novel and then think about the questions below and the key quotes in bold.

> 'Well, Curley's pretty handy,' the swamper said skeptically. 'Never did seem right to me. S'pose Curley jumps a big guy an' licks him. Ever'body says what a game guy Curley is.'...
>
> ...The swamper stood up from his box. 'Know what I think?' George did not answer. 'Well, I think Curley's married ... a tart.'
> 'He ain't the first,' said George. 'There's plenty done that.'

 Think About It

1 What sort of personal belongings might the ranch workers have if there are only two small shelves for each of them (page 13)?

2 The boss is suspicious of George and Lennie because they travel around together. What does this tell you about the other workers on the ranch?

3 Why does Candy want George to say something critical about Curley?

4 'Well – she got the eye.'

Candy suggests that Curley's wife has already been looking around for other men, especially Slim and Carlson. George says that if she is flirting with other men, then that's why 'Curley's pants is full of ants', i.e. he is unsettled and restless because he is unsure of her.

5 'Slim's a jerkline skinner.'

Slim is a skilled wagon driver who controls the team of mules. Candy says he is 'Hell of a nice fella', who doesn't need – like Curley – to wear high-heeled boots. We haven't met Slim yet but he is already being presented as a man to admire. (See page 21 where he is described in more detail.)

Look, Lennie! This here ain't no set up. I'm scared. You gonna have trouble with that Curley. I seen that kind before. He figures he's got you scared and he's gonna take a sock at you the first chance he gets.

I don't want no trouble. Don't let him sock me, George.

If he tangles with you, Lennie, we're gonna get the can. He's the boss's son.

Keep away from him. Don't never speak to him.

Don't let him pull you in — but — if the son-of-a-bitch socks you — let 'im have it. I'll tell you when.

If you get in any trouble, you remember what I told you to do?

If I get in any trouble, you ain't gonna let me tend the rabbits.

That's not what I meant. You remember where we slep' last night?

Yeah, I remember. Oh, sure I remember. I go there an' hide in the brush.

Hide till I come for you. Don't let nobody see you.

If you get in trouble.

- Notice how often the word 'trouble' is used in this conversation. Do you think Lennie will be able to avoid trouble on the ranch?

19

Both men glanced up, for a rectangle of sunshine in the doorway was cut off.

I'm lookin' for Curley.

You're the new fellas that just come, ain't ya?

Sometimes Curley's in here.

Well, he ain't now.

Nobody can't blame a person for lookin'.

Jesus, what a **tramp**. So that's what Curley picks for a wife.

Gosh, she was purty.

Listen to me. Don't you even look at that bitch. I seen 'em poison before, but I never seen no piece of **jail bait** worse than her.

I never done nothing, George.

No, but you wasn't lookin' the other way, neither.

I don' like this place, George. This ain't no good place. I wanna get outa here.

tramp — tart
jail bait — a young woman or girl who flirts and gets men into trouble

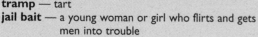 • What makes Lennie think the ranch isn't a 'good place'?

We gotta keep it till we get **a stake**. We'll get out jus' as soon as we can.

I don't like it no better than you do.

Let's go, George. Le's get outa here. It's mean here.

We gotta stay. Shut up now. The guys'll be comin' in.

A tall man stood in the doorway.

He moved into the room, and he moved with a majesty only achieved by royalty and master craftsmen. He was a jerkline skinner, the **prince of the ranch**, capable of driving even twenty mules with a single line to the leaders. There was a **gravity** in his manner and a quiet so profound that all talk stopped when he spoke. His authority was so great that his word was taken on any subject, be it politics or love. His ear heard more than was said to him, and his slow speech had overtones not of thought, but of understanding beyond thought.

a stake — some savings

prince of the ranch — most important worker
gravity — seriousness

He looked kindly at the two in the bunk house.

You the new guys?

You guys ever bucked any barley?

I ain't nothing to scream about, but that big bastard there can put up more grain alone than most pairs can.

You guys travel around together?

We kinda look after each other. Nice fella, but he ain't bright. I've knew him for a long time.

Ain't many guys travel around together. I don't know why. Maybe ever'body in the whole damned world is scared of each other.

It's a lot nicer to go round with a guy you know.

Hi, Slim.

These guys jus' come.

Glad to meet ya. My name's Carlson.

Meant to ask you, Slim — how's your bitch? I seen she wasn't under your wagon this morning.

She **slang** her pups last night.

Why'n't you get Candy to shoot his old dog and give him one of the pups?

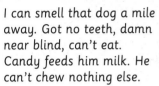

I can smell that dog a mile away. Got no teeth, damn near blind, can't eat. Candy feeds him milk. He can't chew nothing else.

A triangle began to ring outside, slowly at first, and then faster and faster. There was a burst of voices as a group of men went by. Slim stood up slowly and with dignity.

Come on while they's still something to eat.

Yeah! I heard him, Lennie. I'll ask him.

A brown and white one!

The two of them started for the door. Just as they reached it, Curley bounced in.

You seen a girl around here?

'Bout half an hour ago maybe. She was lookin' for you.

Which way'd she go?

I dunno. I didn' watch her go.

Ya know, Lennie, I'm scared I'm gonna tangle with that bastard myself. I hate his guts.

slang — gave birth to

triangle — rung by the cook to tell the men a meal is ready

23

| 3 | Slim gives Lennie a puppy, and George tells him about their friendship. Candy's old dog is shot but he offers his savings to George to help to buy a small farm. Curley attacks Lennie. |

Although there was evening brightness showing through the windows of the bunk house, inside it was dusk. Through the open door came the thuds and occasional clangs of a horseshoe game.

Slim and George came into the bunk house together.

I don't know how we're gonna get him to sleep in here. He'll want to sleep in the barn with 'em.

It wasn't nothing. No need to thank me.

It wasn't much to you, maybe, but it was a hell of a lot to him.

Say, you sure was right about him. I never seen such a worker. There ain't nobody can keep up with him. I never seen such a strong guy.

Funny how you an' him string along together.

Oh, I dunno. I hardly never seen two guys travel together. You know how the **hands** are, they just come in and work a month and then they quit and go out alone. Never seem to give a damn about nobody.

What's funny about it?

hands — ranch workers

24

I knowed his Aunt Clara. She took him in when he was a baby. When his Aunt Clara died, Lennie just come along with me out workin'. Got kinda used to each other after a little while.

Used to play jokes on 'im. Made me seem smart alongside of him. He'd do any damn thing I tol' him.

Tell you what made me stop that. A bunch of guys was standin' around up on the Sacramento River. I was feelin' pretty smart. I turns to Lennie and says, 'Jump in.' An' he jumps. Couldn't swim a stroke. Damn near drowned. An' he was so damn nice to me for pullin' him out.

He's a nice fella. Guys don't need no sense to be a nice fella.

I ain't got no people. I seen the guys that go around on the ranches alone. They don't have no fun. They get mean.

Yeah. They get so they don't want to talk to nobody.

Course Lennie's a God damn nuisance most of the time. But you get used to goin' around with a guy.

I can see Lennie ain't a bit mean.

Course he ain't mean. But he gets in trouble alla time because he's so God damn dumb.

 • How has George's attitude to Lennie changed over the years?

Lennie came in. He walked hunched over.

Lennie. I tol' you you couldn't bring that pup in here.

What pup, George? I ain't got no pup.

George went quickly to him. He reached down and picked the tiny puppy from where Lennie had been concealing it against his stomach.

He's gotta sleep with his mother. Get him back there quick, and don't you take him out no more. You'll kill him, the first thing you know.

Lennie fairly scuttled out of the room.

Jesus. He's jes' like a kid, ain't he?

Sure. There ain't no more harm in him than a kid, except he's so strong.

It was almost dark outside now. Candy came in and went to his bunk, and behind him struggled his old dog. Carlson came in. He sniffed the air, and looked down at the old dog.

He ain't no good to you Candy. An' he ain't no good to himself. Whyn't you shoot him?

I had him so long. I herded sheep with him. No, I couldn't do that.

 • How does George know that Lennie has the puppy with him?

I'll shoot him for you. Then it won't be you that does it.

I'm so used to him. I had him from a pup.

You ain't bein' kind to him keepin' him alive.

I bet Slim would give you one of them pups.

Yeah, you can have a pup if you want to.

Carl's right, Candy. That dog ain't no good to himself. I wish't somebody'd shoot me if I get old an' a cripple.

Maybe it'd hurt him.

The way I'd shoot him he wouldn't feel nothing. Back of the head.

You ain't got no gun.

The hell I ain't. Got a **Luger**. It won't hurt him none at all.

Maybe tomorra. Le's wait till tomorra.

I don't see no reason for it. Let's get it over with.

Luger — a German automatic pistol

Read the following passage of text in your copy of the novel and then think about the questions below and the key quotes in bold.

> " Candy looked a long time at Slim to try to find some reversal. And Slim gave him none. At last Candy said softly and hopelessly, 'Awright – take 'im.' He did not look down at the dog at all. He lay on his bunk and crossed his arms behind his head and stared at the ceiling. ...
>
> ...A shot sounded in the distance. The men looked quickly at the old man. Every head turned toward him.
> For a moment he continued to stare at the ceiling. Then he rolled slowly over and faced the wall and lay silent. "

 Think About It

1 'Seems like Curley ain't givin' nobody a chance.'

How does Candy think that Curley always 'wins' in a fight because of his size? Curley doesn't need to care about what the workers think of him. He will never get 'canned' (sacked) because he is the boss's son.

2 'Maybe he's showin' off for his wife.'

Curley is trying to impress his new wife by bossing the workers about. He is also trying to impress the workers with the fact that he *has* a wife and they don't. When he tells about keeping one hand soft for his wife, he is gloating about having a wife when the others don't.

3 Why is Slim surprised that George and Lennie travel together (**'Funny how you an' him string along together'**, page 24)?

4 How does Slim come to realise that Lennie, although strong, is not mean (page 25)?

5 Why does Candy not look at his dog? We are told five times that Candy stares at the ceiling – why is this important? At the end of the extract he turns to face the wall. Why?

6 Why does Slim tell Carlson to take a shovel?

7 Look at the words used to describe the actions of the men – 'apologetically' (Carlson), 'shortly' (Slim), 'gently' (George), 'loudly' (Slim), 'nervously' (George). They are all uncomfortable and look down to the gnawing sound of the rat 'gratefully' because it allows them to change the subject.

8 Look at how many times the words 'silent' or 'silence' are used in the passage. The emphasis on the silence brings home the men's discomfort about the shooting of the dog but also the anticipation of a particular noise – the gunshot. Candy is 'silent' throughout.

Candy overhears George telling Lennie about their dream of owning their own place. Perhaps with his help that dream can come true.

The door opened quietly and the stable buck put in his head; a lean negro head, lined with pain, the eye patient.

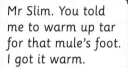

Mr Slim. You told me to warm up tar for that mule's foot. I got it warm.

Oh! Sure, Crooks. I'll come right out an' put it on.

Seen the new kid yet? Curley's new wife. Ain't she a **looloo**?

I ain't seen that much of her.

Stick around. You'll see plenty. She got the eye goin' all the time on everybody. Seems like she can't keep away from guys.

She's gonna make a mess. She's jail bait. That Curley got his work cut out for him.

You ought to come in town with us guys tomorra night.

Why? What's doin'?

Jus' the usual thing. We go in to **old Susy's place**.

Me an' Lennie's rollin' up a stake. I might go and have **a shot**.

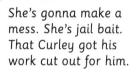

looloo — beauty

old Susy's place — a brothel
shot — glass of whisky

29

The door opened and Lennie and Carlson came in together. Lennie crept to his bunk and lay down, trying not to attract attention. Carlson brought out the pistol and fell to cleaning the barrel.

Curley burst into the room.

Any you guys seen my wife?

She ain't been here.

Where the hell's Slim?

Went out in the barn.

Curley jumped out the door and banged it after him.

I'd like to see this.

Thinks Slim's with his wife, don't he?

I guess I'll go out and **look her over**.

George, how long's it gonna be till we get that little place an' live on the fatta the lan' — an' rabbits?

I don't know. We gotta get a big stake together. I know a little place we can get cheap.

Tell about that place, George. Go on — tell again.

look her over — see what's going to happen

Well, it's ten acres. Got a little shack on it, an' a chicken run. Got a kitchen, orchard. They's a place for **alfalfa** and plenty water. We'd belong there. No more runnin' round the country. We wouldn't have to buck no barley eleven hours a day.

An' rabbits. An' I'd take care of 'em. They'd nibble an' they'd nibble, the way they do. I seen 'em.

You know where's a place like that? How much they want?

I could get it for six hundred bucks.

Say — what's it to you? You got nothing to do with us.

I lost my right hand here. They gave me two hundred an' fifty dollars.

I got fifty more saved up in the bank. S'pose I went in with you guys. I ain't much good but I could cook and hoe the garden some.

I gotta think about that. We was always gonna do it by ourselves.

I'd make a will an' leave my share to you guys in case I **kick off**, 'cause I ain't got no relatives.

alfalfa — a type of grass grown as animal feed
kick off — die

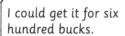

If me an' Lennie work a month an' don't spend nothing I bet we could **swing her** for that.

Then you an' Lennie could go get her started an' I'd get a job an' make up the res'.

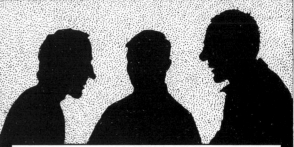

They fell into a silence. They looked at one another, amazed. This thing they had never really believed in was coming true.

I got hurt four year ago. They'll can me purty soon. You seen what they done to my dog? When they can me I wisht somebody'd shoot me.

When we gon'ta do it, George?

Right squack in one month. I'm gon'ta write to them old people that owns the place.

I ought to have shot that dog myself, George. I shouldn't ought to have let no stranger shoot my dog.

swing her — do the deal

The door opened. Slim came in, followed by Curley and Carlson and Whit.

If you can't look after your own God damn wife, what you expect me to do about it?

I'm jus' tryin' to tell you I didn't mean nothing.

You God damn punk. You tried to throw a scare into Slim, an' you couldn't make it stick. You're **yella** as a frog belly.

 Think About It

1 What is your reaction to the killing of Candy's dog? Should Slim have let it happen?

2 Why does Candy say that he ought to have shot his dog himself?

3 It looks as though George and Lennie's dream might actually come true! Do you think it will?

yella — yellow (cowardly)

> Curley attacks Lennie and beats him viciously until George tells Lennie to defend himself.

Read the following passage of text in your copy of the novel and then think about the questions below and the key quotes in bold.

> **"** Candy joined the attack with joy. 'Glove fulla Vaseline,' he said disgustedly. Curley glared at him. His eyes slipped on past and lighted on Lennie; and Lennie was still smiling with delight at the memory of the ranch. ...
>
> ...Suddenly Lennie let go his hold. He crouched cowering against the wall. 'You tol' me to, George,' he said miserably. **"**

 Think About It

1 Look again at page 30. What do the descriptions of how Curley enters and leaves the room tell you about his mood?

2 Why does Curley attack Lennie instead of one of the other (smaller) men? Look back at the passage of text referred to on page 19 where Candy says Curley 'ain't givin' nobody a chance.' We can see the truth of Candy's assessment of Curley here.

3 Two similes are used to describe Curley in this extract. **'Curley stepped over to Lennie like a terrier.'** What does this suggest about his willingness to fight?

'The next minute Curley was flopping like a fish on a line ...' What does this suggest about his helplessness now?

Lennie is also compared to animals: **'Lennie covered his face with his huge paws and bleated with terror.'**

The metaphor 'paws' suggests that he is like a bear (in size and strength) but 'bleated' suggests that he is like a lamb (in fear and emotional weakness).

4 **'Lennie looked helplessly at George.'**

Lennie looks to George for a lead throughout this incident. He tries to retreat, asks George to stop Curley, then responds to George's repeated instruction to 'get him'. Once Lennie has Curley in his grip, however, he finds it hard to listen to George's instruction to 'Leggo' (let go), just like he found it hard to let go of the girl in Weed's dress. Later in the story (the passage referred to on page 46) he also finds it hard to let go, with tragic consequences.

We got to get him to a doctor. Looks like ever' bone in his hand is bust.

I didn't wanta. I didn't wanta hurt him.

Slim, will we get canned now? We need the stake.

Slim smiled. He knelt down beside Curley.

Listen. I think you got your han' caught in a machine. Get this guy canned and we'll tell ever'body, an' then **will you get the laugh**.

I won't tell.

Slim helped Curley to the door.

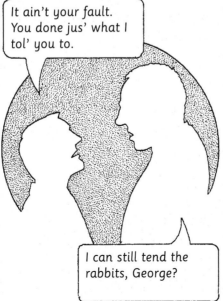

It ain't your fault. You done jus' what I tol' you to.

I can still tend the rabbits, George?

Sure. You ain't done nothing wrong.

Get out and wash your face.

will you get the laugh — you'll look the fool

4	Lennie goes into Crooks' room. At first Crooks is unfriendly, but when Candy joins them and tells him about their plan he asks to join them. Curley's wife arrives and the mood changes.

Crooks, the negro stable buck, had his bunk in the harness-room; a little shed that leaned off the wall of the barn. On one side of the little room there was a square, four-paned window, and on the other, a narrow plank door leading into the barn. Crooks' bunk was a long box filled with straw, on which his blankets were flung. On the walls were pegs from which hung broken harness in process of being mended.

Scattered about the floor were a number of personal possessions; for, being a stable buck and a cripple, he was more permanent than the other men.

Crooks was a proud, **aloof** man. He kept his distance and demanded that other people kept theirs.
It was Saturday night. Crooks sat on his bunk. In one hand he held a bottle of **liniment**, and with the other he rubbed his spine.

aloof — separate/keeps himself to himself
liniment — liquid for rubbing on aches and pains

Noiselessly, Lennie appeared in the open doorway and stood there, looking in. For a moment Crooks did not see him, but on raising his eyes he stiffened and a scowl came on his face.

You got no right to come in my room. This here's my room. Nobody got any right in here but me.

I ain't doing nothing. Just come to look at my puppy. And I seen your light.

I got a right to have a light. Get outta my room. I ain't wanted in the bunk house, and you ain't wanted in my room.

Why ain't you wanted?

'Cause I'm black. They play cards in there but I can't play because I'm black.

Ever'body went into town. George says I gotta stay here an' not get into no trouble.

Long as you won't get out and leave me alone, you might as well set down.

All the boys gone into town, huh?

All but Candy. He just sets in the bunk house **figuring**.

figuring — calculating/working out something

What's Candy figuring about?

The rabbits we're gonna get, and I get to tend 'em.

Jus' nuts. I don't blame the guy you travel with for keeping' you outta sight.

It ain't no lie. We're gonna do it. Gonna get a little place an' live on the fatta the lan'.

You travel around' with George, don't ya? Sometimes he talks, and you don't know what the hell he's talking' about. Ain't that so?

Yeah... sometimes.

I seen it over an' over — a guy talkin' to another guy and it don't make no difference if he don't hear or understand. The thing is, they're talkin'. Jus' bein' with another guy. That's all.

S'pose George don't come back no more. S'pose he gets killed or hurt so he can't come back.

George won't do nothing like that. George is careful.

Jus' s'pose he don't. What'll you do then?

What you doin'? This ain't true. George ain't got hurt.

Want me to tell ya what'll happen? They'll take ya to the **booby hatch**. They'll tie ya up with a collar, like a dog.

booby hatch — lunatic asylum/mental hospital

• Why is Crooks being so cruel to Lennie?

38

Who hurt George?

I was just supposin'. George ain't hurt. He'll be back all right.

Maybe you can see now. You got George. You know he's goin' to come back. S'pose you didn't have nobody. S'pose you couldn't go into the bunk house and play **rummy** 'cause you was black. How'd you like that?

A guy needs somebody — to be near him. A guy goes nuts if he ain't got nobody.

I remember when I was a little kid on my old man's chicken ranch. Had two brothers. They was always near me.

George says we're gonna have rabbits an' a berry patch.

You're nuts. I see hundreds of men come by on the road an' on the ranches with that same damn thing in their heads. They come, an' they quit an' go on; an' every damn one of 'em's got a little piece of land in his head. An' never a God damn one of 'em ever gets it.

Just like heaven. Nobody never gets to heaven, and nobody never gets no land. It's just in their head.

rummy — a card game

Candy stood in the doorway. He made no attempt to enter.

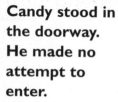
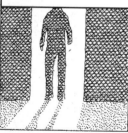

Come on in. If ever'body's comin' in, you might just as well.

Nice cosy little place. Must be nice to have a room all to yourself this way.

Sure, and a manure pile under the window. Sure, it's swell.

About them rabbits.

I got figured out. We can make some money on them rabbits.

You guys is just kiddin' yourself. You won't get no land.

You God damn right we're gonna do it. We got the money right now.

You say you got the money?

Damn right. Just a little bit more to get. Have it all in one month.

I never seen a guy really do it. I seen guys nearly crazy with loneliness for land, but ever' time a whore house or a **blackjack** game took what it takes.

If you... guys would want a hand to work for nothing – just his keep, why I'd come an' lend a hand.

blackjack — a card game

40

Any you boys seen Curley?

Curley ain't been here.

Maybe you better go along to your own house. We don't want no trouble.

I ain't giving you no trouble. Think I don't like to talk to somebody ever' once in a while? Think I like to stick in that house alla time?

Sat'iday night. Ever'body out doin' som'pin. An' what am I doin'? Standin' here talking' to a nigger, a dum dum and a lousy ol' sheep —

an' likin' it because they ain't nobody else.

I had enough. You ain't wanted here. We ain't got nothing to say to you. Curley ain't gonna like his wife out in the barn with us.

Where'd you get them bruises on your face?

He got his han' caught in a machine.

OK, Machine. I'll talk to you later. I like machines.

You let this guy alone.

I had enough. You got no rights comin' in a colored man's room.

• Why does Curley's wife flirt with Lennie?

41

Listen, Nigger. You know what I can do if you open your trap? I could get you **strung up** in a tree so easy it ain't even funny.

Yes, ma'am.

I'm glad you bust up Curley. He got it comin' to him.

She slipped out the door.

That bitch didn't ought to of said that to you.

It wasn't nothing. What she says is true.

Lennie. You in the barn?

Here, George. I'm right in here.

What you doin' in Crooks' room. You hadn't ought to be in here.

I di'n't care much. Lennie's a nice fella.

Well, you guys get outta here.

Candy! 'Member what I said? Well, jus' forget it. I didn't mean it. Jus' foolin'. I wouldn't want to go to no place like that.

The three men went out the door. Crooks sat down on his bunk and looked at the door for a moment, and then reached for the liniment bottle.

strung up — lynched (hanged without a trial)
• How could Curley's wife get Crooks killed?

• Why does Crooks say that he isn't interested in joining in the plan to buy a small farm now?

5 Lennie is alone in the barn with his dead puppy. Curley's wife comes in and tells him about her unhappy life and her own dream. She asks Lennie to stroke her hair, but he panics and accidentally kills her.

It was Sunday afternoon. The sun sliced in through the cracks of the barn walls and lay in bright lines on the hay. From outside came the clang of horseshoes on the playing peg and the shouts of men. But in the barn it was quiet and lazy and warm.

Only Lennie was in the barn. Lennie sat in the hay and looked at the little dead puppy that lay in front of him.

Why do you got to get killed? You ain't so little as mice. I didn't bounce you hard. Now maybe George ain't gonna let me tend no rabbits.

This ain't no bad thing like I got to go hide in the brush. This ain't. I'll tell George I foun' it dead.

What you got there, sonny boy?

George says I ain't to have nothing to do with you — talk to you or nothing.

Why can't I talk to you? I never get to talk to nobody. I get awful lonely. Can't talk to nobody but Curley. Else he gets mad.

George's scared I'll get into trouble.

What you got covered up there?

Jus' my pup. I was jus' playin' with him. An' then he was dead.

Don't you worry none. He was jus' a mutt. You can get another one easy.

George said if I done any more bad things he ain't gonna let me tend the rabbits.

If George sees me talking' to you he'll give me hell. He tol' me so.

What's the matter with me? Ain't I got a right to talk to nobody? Whatta they think I am, anyways? I ain't doin' no harm.

George says you'll get us in a mess.

Nuts! Seems like they ain't none of them cares how I gotta live.

I ain't used to livin' like this. I coulda made somethin' of myself. Maybe I will yet.

I met a guy, an' he was in pitchers. He says he was gonna put me in the movies. Soon's he got back to Hollywood he was gonna write to me.

I never got that letter. I always thought my ol' lady stole it.

So I married Curley. I ain't told this to nobody before. I don't like Curley. He ain't a nice fella.

Coulda been in the movies, an' had nice clothes. An' I coulda sat in them big hotels, an' had pitchers took of me.

Maybe if I took this pup out and throwed him away George wouldn't know. Then I could tend the rabbits.

Don't you think of nothing but rabbits?

I like to pet nice things with my fingers, sof' things.

Who don't? I like to feel silk and velvet. Do you like to feel velvet?

You bet, by God. A lady gave me some — Aunt Clara. I wish't I had that velvet right now. I lost it.

Read the following passage of text in your copy of the novel and then think about the questions below and the key quotes in bold.

> " Curley's wife laughed at him. 'You're nuts,' she said. 'But you're a kinda nice fella. Jus' like a big baby. But a person can see kinda what you mean. When I'm doin' my hair sometime I jus' set an' stroke it 'cause it's so soft.'...
>
> ...He lifted her arm and let it drop. For a moment he seemed bewildered. And then he whispered in fright, 'I done a bad thing. I done another bad thing.' "

 Think About It

1 Curley's wife says that she 'ain't doin' no harm' being in the barn with Lennie (page 44). Is that true?

2 Do you think there ever was a letter from the man in Hollywood?

3 If she doesn't like Curley, why do you think she married him? What is Curley's wife's dream?

4 **'Lennie's fingers closed on her hair and hung on.'**

Look back at the passages referred to on page 9 and page 34 for two other examples of Lennie holding on and not letting go (girl's dress in Weed, Curley's hand and now Curley's wife's hair).

5 Curley's wife talks about her fine hair 'complacently' – she is pleased with herself. Then when she thinks her hairstyle is going to be messed up she cries out 'angrily'. This is very quickly followed by her struggling 'violently'. Her reactions to Lennie have changed very quickly from laughing kindly at him to her eyes being 'wild with terror' as she realises what she has unleashed.

6 **'...her body flopped like a fish. And then she was still, for Lennie had broken her neck.'**

When Lennie crushed Curley's hand he 'flopped like a fish on a line' (see the passage referred to on page 34). This time, more than a hand has been broken.

7 **'I done another bad thing.'**

Is Lennie fully aware of what he has done? He has worried about George being 'mad' and 'He ain't gonna let me tend no rabbits' but he is 'bewildered' when he lifts Curley's wife's arm and lets it drop.

George'll be mad. An'.... an' hide in the brush till he come. He's gonna be mad.

He crept around the end of the last **manger** and disappeared.

As happens sometimes, a moment settled and hovered and remained for more than a moment. And sound stopped for much, much more than a moment. Then gradually time awakened again and moved sluggishly on.

Lennie! You in here? I been figuring some more.

Oh, Jesus Christ!

Candy looked about helplessly and then he went quickly out of the barn.

In a moment Candy came back, and George was with him.

What done it?

I should of knew. I guess maybe I did.

Guess... we gotta tell the... guys. We can't let 'im get away. Why, the poor bastard'd starve. Maybe they'll lock him up an' be nice to 'im.

We oughtta let 'im get away. Curley gon'ta wanta get 'im lynched.

manger — a feeding trough for animals

● Why does Steinbeck suggest that time stood still for a moment at this point in the story?

You an' me can get that little place, can't we, George?

I think I know'd we'd never do her.

Then — it's all off?

I didn't think he'd do nothing like this.

Lennie never done it in meanness.

I ain't gonna let them hurt Lennie. Now you listen. I'm gonna go in the bunk house. In a minute you come out and tell the guys. Will you do that? So the guys won't think I was in on it?

Candy watched him go. He looked back at Curley's wife.

You God damn tramp. Ever'body know'd you'd mess things up.

His eyes blinded with tears and he turned and went out of the barn. Outside the noise of the game stopped. There was a rise of voices, a drum of running feet and the men burst into the barn. Last of all came George.

That big son-of-a-bitch done it. I'm going for my shotgun. I'll kill the son-of-a-bitch.

I'll get my Luger.

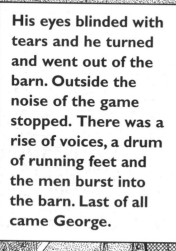

• Is Candy fair to put the blame for what has happened on Curley's wife?

I guess Lennie done it. Her neck's bust.

I guess we gotta get 'im.

Couldn' we maybe bring him in an' they'll lock him up? He's nuts, Slim. He never done this to be mean.

We might. But Curley's gonna want to shoot 'im.

An' s'pose they lock him up an' strap him down and put him in a cage. That ain't no good, George.

The bastard's stole my Luger. It ain't in my bag.

The nigger's got a shotgun. You take it, Carlson.

Listen, Curley. The poor bastard's nuts. Don't shoot 'im. He didn't know what he was doin'.

Don't shoot 'im? He got Carlson's Luger. 'Course we'll shoot 'im.

I'm gonna shoot the guts outta that big bastard myself. I'm gonna get 'im.

When they were gone, Candy lay down in the hay and covered his eyes with his arm.

● What might Slim be suggesting here as an alternative to a mental hospital/prison for Lennie?

6	Lennie has returned to the campsite by the pool. He is terrified that George will leave him now. George arrives before Curley and the others.

The deep green pool was still in the late afternoon. A water snake glided up to the legs of a motionless heron that stood in the shallows. A silent beak lanced down and plucked and swallowed the little snake. Lennie appeared as silently as a creeping bear.

He knelt down and drank.

I di'nt forget, you bet, God damn. Hide in the brush an' wait for George. George gonna give me hell. George gonna wish he was alone an' not have me botherin' him.

Out of Lennie's head came a little old woman. She stood in front of Lennie and frowned disapprovingly at him. And when she spoke, it was in Lennie's voice.

I tol' you an' tol' you. You never give a thought to George. He coulda had a good time if it wasn't for you.

Aunt Clara was gone, and from out of Lennie's head there came a gigantic rabbit. It sat on its haunches in front of him. And it spoke in Lennie's voice too.

If you think George gonna let you tend rabbits, you're crazier'n usual. He's gonna go away an' leave you.

- Why has Steinbeck included a description here of the water snake being killed?

He ain't, I tell ya he ain't. Oh. George — George!

George came quietly out of the brush and the rabbit scuttled back into Lennie's brain.

What the hell you yellin' about?

You ain't gonna leave me, George?

No.

I done another bad thing.

It don't make no difference.

Ain't ya gonna give me hell?

No.

Tell me like you done before. 'Bout the other guys an' about us.

Tell about us.

George took off his hat.

Take off your hat, Lennie. The air feels fine.

Tell how it's gonna be.

Look acrost the river, Lennie, an' I'll tell you so you can almost see it.

• Why does Lennie want George to repeat their 'dream'? Why does George agree to repeat it?

51

Read the following passage of text in your copy of the novel and then think about the questions below and the key quotes in bold.

> **"** Lennie turned his head and looked off across the pool and up the darkening slopes of the Gabilans. 'We gonna get a little place,' George began. He reached in his side pocket and brought out Carlson's Luger; ...
>
> ...He pulled the trigger. The crash of the shot rolled up the hills and rolled down again. Lennie jarred, and then settled slowly forward to the sand, and he lay without quivering. **"**

 Think About It

1 Why isn't George angry with Lennie?

2 **'Look down there across the river, like you can almost see the place.'**

George describes the dream for one last time to Lennie. It is as if he is describing heaven, or the Promised Land. **'Ever'body gonna be nice to you. Ain't gonna be no more trouble.'**

3 'A man's voice called from up the river and another man answered.'
'There were crashing footsteps in the bush now.'
'The voices came close now.'
The scene between George and Lennie is about to be disturbed at any moment. The noises from the outside world make us anxious for Lennie. Will he escape the lynch mob?

4 **'The crash of the shot rolled up the hills and rolled down again.'**

Compare this to (page 28) 'A shot sounded in the distance' when Candy's dog was shot. The men were ashamed. George is shooting Lennie while he is at one with nature and looking towards his dream place. He has no need to be ashamed. He is doing what is best for Lennie, whose end is peaceful.

George shivered and looked at the gun, and then he threw it from him. The brush seemed filled with cries and the sounds of running feet. The group burst into the clearing, and Curley was ahead.

Got him, by God. Right in the back of the head.

Never you mind. A guy got to sometimes.

Did he have my gun?

Yeah. He had your gun.

An' you got it away from him and you took it an' you killed him.

Yeah. That's how.

Come on, George. Me an' you'll go in an' get a drink.

Yeah, a drink.

You hadda, George. I swear you hadda. Come on with me.

Now what the hell ya suppose is eatin' them two guys?

The End

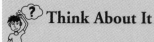 **Think About It**

1 What similarities have you noticed between the shooting of Candy's dog and the shooting of Lennie?

2 Look again at what Slim said on page 49. Do you think he knows the truth of what has happened?

3 In the full text, Curley sends Whit to fetch the deputy sheriff from Soledad. What do you think will happen when he arrives?

4 As the title of the book suggests, all George's plans have come to nothing. What do you think the future now holds for George and the other characters?

5 Some people have criticised the way George 'saves' Lennie by shooting him. They do not agree with 'euthanasia' (mercy killing). What do you think?